T0290185

The Hands

ESSENTIAL POETS SERIES 294

ONTARIO ARTS COUNCIL
CONSEIL DES ARTS DE L'ONTARIO

an Ontario government agency
un organisme du gouvernement de l'Ontario

Canada Council   Conseil des arts
for the Arts   du Canada

Guernica Editions Inc. acknowledges the support of
the Canada Council for the Arts and the Ontario Arts Council.
The Ontario Arts Council is an agency of the Government of Ontario.
We acknowledge the financial support of the Government of Canada

Marty Gervais

The Hands

GUERNICA
EDITIONS

TORONTO • CHICAGO • BUFFALO • LANCASTER (U.K.)
2022

Guernica Founder: Antonio D'Alfonso

Michael Mirolla, general editor
Bruce Meyer, editor
Cover and Interior Design: Rafael Chimicatti
Guernica Editions Inc.
287 Templemead Drive, Hamilton (ON), Canada L8W 2W4
2250 Military Road, Tonawanda, N.Y. 14150-6000 U.S.A.
www.guernicaeditions.com

Distributors:
Independent Publishers Group (IPG)
600 North Pulaski Road, Chicago IL 60624
University of Toronto Press Distribution (UTP)
5201 Dufferin Street, Toronto (ON), Canada M3H 5T8
Gazelle Book Services
White Cross Mills, High Town, Lancaster LA1 4XS U.K.

First edition.
Printed in Canada.

Legal Deposit – First Quarter
Library of Congress Catalog Card Number: 2021949859
Library and Archives Canada Cataloguing in Publication
Title: The hands / Marty Gervais.
Names: Gervais, C. H. (Charles Henry), 1946- author.
Series: Essential poets ; 294.
Description: First edition.
Series statement: Essential poets series ; 294 | Poems.
Identifiers: Canadiana 20210364300 | ISBN 9781771837286 (softcover)
Classification: LCC PS8563.E7 H36 2022 | DDC C811/.54—dc23

Contents

Introduction: A Show of Hands | 9

Prologue

Making the Difference: Gustavo Gutiérrez | 17

Language at the River

COVID Language at the River | 21

Peoples Along the South Shore | 22

Confederation Day, July 1, 1867: Windsor | 23

Here It Is | 25

Walking Distance | 27

When the Light Gets Warm | 28

Room With a Face | 31

The Light is Never Right | 33

The Cure | 34

Meeting the Dead in May | 37

American Standard | 40

His Father's Work

Dream of the Cottage | 45

Anything More Beautiful | 46

Backyard Workshop | 48

His Father's Work: Manly Miner | 50

Something I Wanted to Say | 53

Tape Machine: Leonard Cohen | 55

Image-making: Paul Martin | 57

Moments Before the Old Presses
Started at the Windsor Star | 59

The Hands

Taking the Picture: Yousuf Karsh | 63

Hands of a Saint: Mother Teresa | 65

Mickey Mantle's Last At Bat at Tiger Stadium | 67

Jimmy Sleeps Alone | 69

On Meeting Benjamin Spock | 71

The Hands: Muhammad Ali | 73

Arthur Miller: Don't Ask? | 75

Tomato Wine | 77

Postcard from Paris:
    Afternoon with Mavis Gallant | 79

Joni Mitchell's Bed | 80

Walking in Thomas Merton's Boots | 81

Finding the Right Words: Robert Giroux | 82

Sleeping Beauty: Karen Kain | 83

Belonging Somewhere: Rosa Parks | 84

The One Thing that Catches the Eye:
    Mary Ellen Mark | 88

Vladimir Horowitz: The American Tour Resumes
    in Detroit After the Death of His Mother | 89

Epilogue

Obits | 93

Acknowledgements | 94
About the Author | 95

A hand turned upward holds only a single,
transparent question.

—Jane Hirshfield, "A Hand"

Introduction: A Show of Hands

GOOD POETS NOTICE THINGS. They look at the world and, instead of being distracted by the larger canvas of experience, they see how the world is held together. They notice the finer points of people and things. They love the details. Their eyes frame the specific. What they see speaks to both the mind and the heart. That is what poems are made of. Good poets predicate their work on the idea that seeing is believing. They have their eyes open.

The other gift bestowed on successful poets is the ability to connect what the poet sees to the humanity of what it sees. A hand is not a hand, but something that is part of a person, inseparable from the body that owns it. And what the poet sees and records and remembers is what speaks to the human condition. Aristotle would have called this "ethos" – the information that connects us to each other and shapes what we know and desire. The poet says, "This is what I see, and what I see is important to who a person is because what they do, what they hold onto in life informs the essence of their being."

Without either of these gifts, a poem falls flat. All the language in the world cannot save a poem that attempts to articulate an important moment in the human experience if the poet doesn't empathize with the subject matter. Great poems not only remind us who we are. Great poems tug at us to recognize that who we are is important to the world because what we say or do, touch or feel, receive, and give create the persona we present to the world. A river, for instance, in poems such as "Language of the River," or "The People Along the South Shore," are brought together through the common bond of language. Language is not merely the words one speaks, but the way the world speaks to us. The poet's job is to listen to the world, record and interpret what it says, and recount it with humanity and grace and charm and ethos to tell us the story not merely of the river but of ourselves. So much of the world wants to speak to us, and one of the great pities is that we don't stop to listen.

If a poet is a good listener, he listens not only to the stories he encounters through his eyes. He listens with his eyes. And therein resides the purpose of this book. The poems in *Hands* focus on the stories the eye tells us. The author of these poems, Marty Gervais, is not merely an outstanding poet who has tuned his ear and mind to the world or even a reporter who has heard millions of stories in his life and asked far more questions than anyone would think capable to elicit those stories. He is someone who listens to what the world says to him.

To call this form of listening with the eyes 'reading' does the process little justice. In this collection, Gervais introduces us to the people he has met, the stories he has heard, and the stories he has seen as an established and articulate photographer, to remind us that everything is a story.

The epigraph to this collection, a phrase from the photographer Jane Hirshfield, describes what a poem does. A poem contains both the visible elements of imagery and something else that is difficult to give a name to. Is it the unseen? Perhaps. Is it the spirit of the person being photographed or the moment when the waves of a river are caught in suspended animation? Poets have always known this element exists in poetry, the element of the unseen. Perhaps it is faith if one takes the famous maxim from Hebrews 11:1 that faith is the substance of things hoped for and the evidence of things not seen. In many ways, a poem is built around what is not seen. For want of a better term, this is the invisibility factor. It cannot be put into words because it cannot present itself as an image but it is there. It is the energy that makes a poem vital, that captures the idea behind the words, not merely the words or the lines or the stanzas, but those pictures in the mind that declare a moment can last forever. As Shakespeare said in Sonnet 30, it is the element of eternal life: the eternal lines to time in which subject not only is described but grows and takes on a life of its own.

Photography revolutionized poetry before poets understood just how profound and meaningful the captured moment is. The photographer points his lens, releases the shutter that blinks, and in the blink of an eye, albeit a mechanical one, the moment lasts forever. I can imagine that if William Shakespeare was alive today he would be a digital artist armed with the latest camera and lenses, perhaps accompanying Gervais on his forays where he takes pictures of a diverse range of subjects – the abandoned eloquence and fading elegance of old Detroit, the fields of Burgundy in France as the sun is rising, the light along a passageway between buildings in Bologna, and the faces and details of those he has met as a journalist.

This latter group, those whom Gervais interviewed while working as the Religions Editor at the *Windsor Star*, fill the pages of these books. His service to those Gervais encountered was not merely to honour them by writing words about them but to capture the moment in which they existed and spoke and breathed and thought about their answers to his questions. They reside in that moment when they are most human, their minds are so focused on what they want to say they forget who they are. They enter that realm that cannot be named because it is ethereal, the evidence of things not seen cited by Hirshfield in the epigraph.

The opening poem in the book is for Gustavo Gutiérrez, which chronicles Gervais' meeting with a Catholic priest in Lima, Peru. In his biography, Peru holds a special place for Gervais who had been christened Charles Henry Gervais by an uncle who was a priest. Gervais' mother wanted him to be named Douglas. None of the names seemed to fit the affable, kind, editor, poet, and journalist who, on the one hand, is constantly aware of the world and on the other surprised by that element of things not seen. In Peru, the old names vanished.

Impressed by the life and work of the Peruvian saint, Martin de Porres, who dedicated himself to the service of others and aid for the poor, Gervais underwent a sea-change in his personality so that he dedicated his life to learning about others, listening to others, and asking them questions so they could understand themselves by revealing themselves. This is the moment, whether he knew it or not, that the journalist in Gervais was born. The name Marty comes from that Saint Martin and represents who Gervais felt he must be – a man of faith not merely in God but in humanity who has worked tirelessly in the cause of the written word. With the name Marty, he embraced a powerful form of humility that is evident in his interviews with some of the great figures of our age and the photographs he snapped of them. Great icons are real people who by accident or intention do great things.

Some of the icons are personal ones such as his father. Other range from Jimmy Hoffa to Leonard Cohen to Mother Theresa – and as Eliot put in "The Love Song of J. Alfred Prufrock," "for I have known them, known them all." In the gamut of the living and the dead, Gervais treats each one with equal dignity. He describes what they said and did, but what is more important is the way he describes their hands. The eyes are windows to the soul, but hands are the foundations upon which the soul is built. What they choose to hold, the way they hold things, the gentleness of a familiar touch or a handshake with greatness is what makes these poems captivating. They are records of how individuals grasped for life and held on, if only for that fleeting moment when, in the palm of their hands, they held the whole world, or at least enough of it to make us wonder how they held so much even when their hands appear empty to the untrained eye.

Bruce Meyer

PROLOGUE

Making the Difference: Gustavo Gutiérrez

I trailed along with two Catholic missionaries
from Canada who led me to Lima's wide
open Plaza de Armas to meet this middle-aged priest
among the morning bustle of traffic – a man
heralded as the founder of *Liberation Theology*
a radical philosophy blessing the poor for battling
in the streets, fighting the government

yet for this rounded, professorial prelate
it was theory, philosophy, words, prayers, whatever
but *violence?* To this, he merely pursed his lips

and for the longest time, he spoke to me
through a translator, the missionary, who
had brought me there, but shook his head
at the request for an interview –

That all changed when I handed him a cheque
from a Canadian bishop, money for the cause
of *Liberation*, and the philosopher/priest quickly
hunted for his glasses before carefully
putting them on to examine the amount
then cocked his head to one side, and smiled
and for the first time turned to look directly at me
and nodded slowly, and now spoke in perfect English

—no trace of an accent, assuring me
he'd answer all my questions

then eyes reverently rolling up to the heavens above
softly he kissed the cheque in his hand—

LANGUAGE AT THE RIVER

COVID Language at the River

The fishermen gather at the curved shoreline
in Sandwich, praying for silver bass
to find their bait, to fill their baskets

and all through a silent sunny morning
they meditate – this staggered lineup
along the waterfront, only muted gestures

serving as words for those whose lines
are flung into the drift and drag of the river
but the language here is clear and persuasive

in a single purpose to carry on, to live side
by side, ever-present, yet keep the distance
and let the running river keep us one

Peoples Along the South Shore

In spring they planted apple seedlings
hope and a prayer, a life of change
in new land by the river

a new world, theirs in every slope
running down to embrace the water's edge

Now I step on the pathway
pushing through knee-high prairie grass
to greet across the water
factory chimneys with a hallelujah of
puffing smoke, now far from
that moment when they knelt in gratitude
200 years ago after departing France
eager to wake each morning to a sun
so distant from the sea that brought them here

and now the land inhabits that emptiness
but for a single tree a hundred yards
from the twisting river
its skeletal branches
bowing piously in the wind

a few withered apples still clinging
in silent defiance –

hope and a prayer, a life of change

Confederation Day, July 1, 1867: Windsor

There were speeches and 21-gun salutes
and parades and games and
there was drinking –

an effigy of Charles Tupper
burned at Halifax Harbour
alongside a live rat

a roasted ox to feed the poor
at the foot of Toronto's Church Street

and later that night a sky alight
with fireworks over Queen's Park

and a Hamilton girl writing
about a sky full of shooting stars
a fountain of red and green and blue
and a father promising her
she was a very lucky girl
to be a child in Canada today

But here in this river town
with its muddy roads threading out
along a shoreline alive with revellers
and stilt-walkers and
clapboard storefronts draped

with the Union Jack
came redcoats with bayonets
scurrying from nearby barracks

not to celebrate or honour or applaud
but to face a rioting of angry men
who pelted them with rocks

By nightfall, the rioters
– defeated and sad – trundled home
while men and women, swinging lanterns
paraded through darkened streets
marvelling at a ribbon of bonfires
lighting the curved south shore

Yet there still was no mistaking
this summer moon high above this river
turning away in shame
to behold how the streets below
heaved with lament
as club-wielding blacks and whites
marshalled in this new day

Here It Is

On the occasion of the opening of the new City Hall,
Windsor, May 26, 2018

Here it is in a town that runs to the river
a place rising from neighbourhoods and promises
of brick and mortar and words

Here it is taking shape into a poetry
of clean lines stretching skyward with grace

Here it is expecting the meaningfulness
of men and women mingling in its shadows

Here it is in a town that runs to the river
a place elbowing its way into new life
amid the action of words and lofty gestures

Here it is with a pledge to define
and bring us into a new gathering place
of brick and wood and glass

Here it is in a town that runs to the river
guiding us into playful dialogue
inviting us to listen, to open our eyes

Here it is surfacing from the sweep
of huddled neighbourhoods
and urging us to sing of its purpose

Here it is, a gathering spot that's ours
in a town that runs to the river.

Walking Distance

Near twilight in this walk down an alley
grown over with tall grass
and solitary wavering sunlit
Queen Anne's Lace –
I feel the world around me
grow anxious of new routines
weary of unsettling news

yet in trailing down this hopeless
long line of tall rickety wooden fences
garbage cans and discarded tires
I see someone has suspended a teacup
over a delicate plate and it twirls
silently in the fading day
reminding me I am not alone

When the Light Gets Warm

When the light gets warm
the world curves
around the Stoney Point farmhouse
where childhood races in sunlight
disappearing into shadows

I am a boy hiding
on my brothers in the henhouse
peering through chicken wire
to the yard with
its shiny bright Buick
I see them running
trying to find me
I am giggling
and the birds
cautiously step away
like 11-year-old girls
walking in an older sister's
high heels

When the light gets warm
I am a boy squatting
in the henhouse
watching the day wind
down, seeing my family
search behind

farm sheds, silos
and along fence rows
I see my mother pushing
back a lock of hair
one hand on her hip
in worry, my father
pacing beside the car
and lighting up a cigarette
my grandmother coming
from the house, the screen door
slapping behind her
wanting the last word

When the light gets warm
they have given up
and no longer call out
and my father slips into the Buick
slams the door and
my brothers pile in one by one
so does my mother
who glances back
one last time
I feel so alone as
I sit in the henhouse
and wonder at my hands
cupping a heart full of melancholy

knowing summer is
turning to twilight

When the light gets warm
I suddenly burst
from the henhouse
my six-year-old legs
sprinting to the Buick
that is now moving
in a cloud of road dust
and I can smell
the fields of wheat
and hear my tiny voice
rising all the way down
to my beating heart
in my chest
then see a back door
opening and a brother's hand
reaching out …

Room With a Face

The room glows
from a storybook quarter moon
that hangs in the window
and the ghost-white cows far below
doze away in the valley
dreaming of tomorrow's
sunshine and rain

and I fall to sleep
seeing the moon
press its face to the glass
wishing it might join me
in this night of stories

I tell it instead to stay where it is
I tell it to wait and see
I tell it to sing me a lullaby
as I wait to fall away free

The room glows
from a storybook quarter moon
I touch its grimacing face
I feel it depart – graceful
and splendid –
soaring into darkness
so the meadow can bloom full of light

I wish myself to sleep
hearing the moon breathe
I sail with it safely into the night sky
the drifting clouds beneath

The room glows
from a storybook quarter moon
and I feel myself lifting into darkness
my limbs soaring among stars
and glimpsing the house
and slumbering cows
in the sleepy meadow below

I tell the moon to whisper its rumors
I tell it to linger and hear
I tell it to sing of its passage
into a place without fear

The Light is Never Right

The light is never right
and the letters are never large enough
in the book I am reading, and the lines
on the page bleed together
and my index finger no longer confidently
traces the bottom edge of a line

yet still I press on, and that's when
words the writer never intended begin
leaping willy-nilly off the page
like crazed acrobats vying for my attention

The best and the worst of reading
is finding words that are not on the page
– a staggering subtext that betrays
a vastly different story, one never meant
or imagined, yet sometimes makes sense

Other times, I scratch my head
puzzling endlessly over why suddenly
the word "eat" appears in the place of "cat"
yet still I scramble and struggle and somehow
finally find a way to make sense of it

The Cure

I was not quite six years old
and I stepped out onto Ouellette Avenue
trailing my father, my tiny hands shading
my eyes from the dazzling sun
after my very first eye exam

I started wearing glasses two days later
and they rested unnaturally on my nose
like a sparrow dreaming of flying off
somewhere soon –

what followed were years
of schoolyard fights and cracked lenses
snapped temples, broken bridges, missing screws
and my father warning me he'd let me go blind
if I didn't care for them any better

But my brother cooked up a cure
in a comic book from the bodybuilder
Charles Atlas, the man who claimed
to rip up a New York phone book in half
bend an iron rod into a horseshoe shape
with his bare hands, and now boasted
of curing blindness

and so my brother offered to lower me slowly
into the well at my grandfather's farm
near Stoney Point and there I'd slip
into the cold deep expanse, wearing only a bathing suit
open my eyes wide underwater for a minute
and a half – and that's all there was to it

I was terrified – I was 6
my head was swimming in doubts, if the rope
snapped or my brother lost his grip
I couldn't swim, I'd never get out

and so instead he calmly led me to the farmyard
to the well near the chicken coop
and pumped the handle till water gushed
and filled a rounded and wide tin pan
that rested on the ground and told me
to take in a deep deep breath, dip my face
eyes open wide, into the water
and he'd count down the time
for the cure to happen

but he kept pushing my head down
my eyes staring into the scratched surface
of the basin, then finally lifted my face
from the frigid well water, and I scanned

the farmyard, saw the red blur of the hen house
and a zigzagging clothesline wavering
in the windy yard, and my dad's car
near the front steps of the farmhouse

and my brother clowning about nearby
laughing his head off –

I'd wear glasses for the rest of my life

Meeting the Dead in May

You will spend the day visiting the dead

– that's what my mother told me
when she buttoned up my stiff white shirt
affixed a bow tie to the collar …
I wore my brother's hand-me-down pants
and a pair of shiny black shoes.

I was dressed and ready for the dead.

I was probably 5, and I waited patiently
beside my father's Plymouth parked
under the lilacs in bloom
The weather was warm
and my buddy from across the street
ambled over and asked why
I was all dressed up

I told him I was going to meet the dead.

I had never seen a dead body before
except on television –
I was pretty excited

I was dressed and ready

My buddy told me he had seen
his dead uncle last winter – nothing special
He had expected his uncle's eyes
might be gaping, like the cattle-rustlers
on *Gunsmoke* when they lay
in the dusty street in Dodge City
dead at the hands of the righteous
Marshall Matt Dillon

I was dressed and ready
– eyes open or not

That day in early May I'd see two dead
when my father drove to Stoney Point
out to the farm near Lake St. Clair
– the morticians had already been there
with embalming equipment

and the first place we stopped we paused
in the parlour – cousins, and aunts
nodding in silence, barely a whisper when
suddenly a window blind let go and snapped up
and everyone abruptly turned to the deceased
as if they thought he might awaken

I made the sign of the cross –
I was dressed and ready for the dead

The second farm we stopped at down by
the Lighthouse belonged to the deceased –
no wife, no children, a bachelor farmer
and he lay in his coffin in the big kitchen
rosary beads twisted around his stubby fingers
I noticed his nails had been scrubbed clean

and everyone wore black, especially
a collection of gnarly old widows
who looked like witches – bony hands forever
reaching out to pinch my cheeks
and marvelling at the colour

I figured I'd be boiled alive with the apples

I was dressed and ready for the dead

American Standard

The day of the American election
I saw a man dragging a toilet from
an open garage at his house to the edge
of the road, and resting it on the curb
and a few days later I drove by his place
and there was the toilet still sitting
like a bored pre-schooler waiting for his mom
who was terribly late picking him up

and the next day the toilet was still there
patiently waiting for someone – its life
had always been one of waiting
but someone always came, sometimes
at dawn when everyone else was asleep
there'd be someone who wanted him
and they'd arrive and sit for a while
maybe read the paper, maybe have a smoke

and soon many hours later, it would get busy
and many more would stop, some to sit
some to stand, always a silent hello goodbye
and hours would pass and no one would come
and weeks would pass and no one –
but such absences were always broken
by abrupt arrivals, and then one after another
they came and it felt like they missed him

But now he sat alone at the edge of the road
seat down and eager while cars whizzed by
all day long, yet no one came to sit or stand
or lift his seat or say hello, goodbye, or sit
and read a book and smoke, but he was
always ready to serve, and figured that's why
they called him 'American Standard' yet still
no one came, but they would – they always did

HIS FATHER'S WORK

Dream of the Cottage

for my father

In the dream, I am at my father's old cottage
and the lake reminds me of a friend dozing
on a couch, lazy and placid –

and it pleases me that it's the end
of a long afternoon, and the clouds
are calmly drifting in, and the sun

soon will pack up his things and retreat
and I sit on the long porch and wait
for the moon to poke her face into

the last bit of radiance in a darkening sky
and it's the trees circling the lake
that finally fall to sleep, and it is there

in that quietude, the dream takes shape
and I am home again, blessed with doing
nothing more than watching and listening

Anything More Beautiful

I wondered what he was thinking in 1926
when he arrived by train from Cobalt
and found a two-story rooming house
on Albert Road, a street that bore
his first name and he carried a
leather satchel and a few brushes
and canvases and believed he might
yet have a chance of becoming a painter

and thought he might run down
to the library to find books filled with
pictures by European artists he'd only
ever heard about but had only ever
seen in newspapers but there never
was any time for that – he was working
on the line at a factory a mile and a half
from the house he lived in – a bedroom

with a window overlooking a cramped
little garden, and it was now spring
and the magnolia tree was coming alive
and he'd never seen anything more beautiful
and yearned to paint it, and finally one day
sat upstairs in his room, the window
slid full open and he began painting –
the Sunday morning light lifting

its colour awake, and he'd never felt so good
likely not since he was a boy in Cobalt
when he'd wander beyond the town far
from the bewildering network of winding
wooden sidewalks and saloons to charcoal
sketch the last bit of daylight etched
in the rolling hills of the stark and silhouetted
gallows-frames of old silver mines

Backyard Workshop

It was always after supper and always
in the summer and always after
my father had had a couple of beers
and read *The Windsor Daily Star*
that he'd gesture for me to join him
for a ride over to George Avenue

to visit my grandfather and I'd scramble up
on to the patterned broadcloth seats
of the big Chevrolet
I was six or seven then
and we'd make our way along the river
and down George to the two-story house

and I'd sprint from the car and race
through the garden to find my grandfather
in the cramped little shed, the painful whine
of the table saw and him leaning over his work
sleeves rolled up cleanly past the elbows
spectacles nearly slipping off his nose

and he'd turn to us with a broad smile
in a world of saws and chisels and stacks
of boards and a floor covered in wood shavings
and a dangling bare lightbulb above
affording him that last wink of light
at the end of a summer day

and it was there I'd watch and eavesdrop
as he spoke a language I'd never learn
a lexicon I'd never comprehend, words
tumbling out of him as he unravelled
the mysteries of a half-blind dovetail joint
the science of making a perfect doweling

Believe me, it was easier to understand
the Blessed Trinity but here I'd watch
transfixed by these puzzling words, lost
in their rhythmic sounds, and still patiently
marvel at all these pieces coming together
while I surrendered to disbelief, seeing

my grandfather moving with the grace
of an artist yet bringing to life something
as simple and ordinary as a kitchen cabinet
with recessed drawer fronts and doors
and I remember nothing of the how-to
the choice of tools he used or why –

nothing but the steadied refrains
of hammers and saws amid the melodious
and mysterious turns in his voice as he spun
unfathomable secrets before me – it was all
poetry, alive and mesmerizing in summers
at dusk in the workshop behind his house

His Father's Work: Manly Miner

Met him early on a Monday morning –
a stout old man, still sporting bowtie and tweeds
good-natured, jabbering the whole time
as he guided me through his childhood home
– still living there, still sleeping
in the same upstairs windowed bedroom
the wide flat sweep of the farm just beyond

Jack's oldest son carrying on the legend
under the high eaves of the red-bricked home
his father built in 1922 next to the roadside pond

Yet this son was nothing like his father
– better schooled, better at fitting together
the right words, but possessed none of the charm
none of the charisma of the naturalist described
as Billy Sunday of the Birds
a man whose fractured words still somehow
left audiences weeping or laughing

But this son was a believer and put steady faith
in his father's work, dutifully fastening
aluminum leg bands to the geese
each band stamped with scripture texts
each bird now a missionary on a 6,000-mile journey

This fastidious custodian of the legend
the day I met him settled in the parlour happy to chat
– memories of an era when hundreds of cars
lined the roadside outside their sanctuary
memories too of tagging along in Europe
with his father on the lecture circuits

But life now was an easier pace at the sanctuary
with brother Jasper – more the farmer
than the cultured bore – people in Kingsville
called the two the "odd couple"
Manly, like an old-time Methodist cleric
doing all the talking and Jasper racing a motorbike
to scatter the geese for roadside visitors

That Monday, Manly was reminiscing
those years of rising early one morning
to join his father and the Tigers' Ty Cobb
– rifles resting gently on their arms, strolling
lazily into the woods to hunt owls and hawks
or the afternoon when he glanced up
from the paper at the cluttered kitchen table
to see Marilyn Monroe stepping shyly into the room

That day it was different – a gray morning
fog drifting in from the lake
letter-writing for the wildlife foundation
no longer muddling his hours
– the eldest son's biggest worry now
was gathering up his underwear and socks and shirts
for the women in town to pick up and wash

Something I Wanted to Say

I wanted to be him – that man
who arrived every summer
and layered oversized canvasses
over the bow of an aluminum boat
as carefully and delicately balanced
as a teacup and saucer on my mother's lap

and then cranked up the outboard motor
till it sputtered and coughed and finally erupted
like an old man waking in a start
and he'd put-put-put across the lake to the island

a solitary man who came weekends from Toronto
from an office tower, I imagined
from a life that seemed all a lie
to this moment when now he sailed at dusk
to the island and I'd stand at the shore
and stare across to his cabin or swim
in the cool cottage waters and forget
about him entirely until his return

– the aluminum boat sliced
through Muskoka's blue mist Monday mornings
canvases laid out flat over the boat
like a hunter's kill in the Fall
the oils ablaze with colour

I wanted to be him – that man
whose idea of creation was everything I yearned for
the poetry of grace and colour

I wanted to tell him this, and promised I would
but sadly missed him the day he returned

I'd have to wait for next summer or
the summer after or maybe never

Tape Machine: Leonard Cohen

I had only ever seen him once before –
York University in the mid-1960s
He was reading from *Beautiful Losers*
I watched him pause and swivel around
to pick up a guitar, all the time talking
a steady slow stream in a deep voice
and him reaching down again this time
for what looked like a white paper bag
that had been torn at the seams
unfolding it into one long sheet
close enough for me to see
there was writing on it –
I was also surprised by the guitar –
he had not yet recorded anything
and he apologized saying *I just wrote this*
please have patience with me – I'm not sure
it's finished – then came the words lifting off
this paper bag *Suzanne takes you down to her place*
near the river ... You can hear the boats go by
You can spend the night forever ...
first time in public
Years later, I met him in Toronto
expecting someone cool, distant, philosophical
in the Park Plaza hotel suite
the iconic literary figure with a trace
of coyness in his voice and attitude

yet he was more like a kid bouncing
about with a new toy – this spiffy, elegant
shiny, portable tape player in his hands
a broad smile slowly accentuating deep lines
on a perfectly tanned face
handing me headphones to listen – his latest
So, what do you think? he asked with a shrug
Great! I responded instantly
I can't for the life of me remember the song
I was paying more attention to him
watching me listening

Image-making: Paul Martin

Late spring morning, magnolias in bloom
and he was holding a newspaper in one hand
a steaming mug of coffee in the other
strolling in the garden
eager to talk to me
about his return from England
leaving a job as High Commissioner
returning to Walkerville
to write his memoirs

but there was never going be none
of the backroom stuff, amid his dealings
with Mackenzie King, St. Laurent,
Pearson, Trudeau, nothing about how
he really felt about frantic days on the hustings
speeches and ribbon-cutting ceremonies

It was all image – all about appearances –
and certainly nothing of the embarrassment
when he was learning how to drive a car
and got into an accident

It was all image – all about appearances
though now there was nothing to gain, no pressing need
to win an election or trade favours

We chatted about everything but politics
all the while a photographer circled around

It was all image – all about appearances

so the wary politician quickly
smoothed out a satin shirt that was missing buttons
then fastened the last button on his jacket
and sat up straight and struck
that ambassadorial pose
of an august man of refinement –

never for the life of him realizing
this was no head-and-shoulders shot

and he was barefoot

Moments Before the Old Presses
Started at the Windsor Star

The first thing you'd see were
the hands, gloved and ink-stained
then the faces of men dwarfed by
the three-storied leviathan that sprawled out
in the morning ready to rouse and rise
You'd eye the pressmen pacing the perimeter
of this giant and see them stretch long clean sheets
of paper from giant rolls through its idle frame

They knew the monster well and knew
to wait and knew to hear its glory

I used to slide down from the newsroom
to stand nearby and watch, and hear the voices
over the faint growl of this prodigious creature
I'd see them carrying heavy metal plates
clamping them into place, and watching them fit
the curved cylinders to its pulsating contours
catch the slow mumble among
the men as they moved to feed the beast
to make it come alive, to make it stir

They knew the monster well and knew
to wait and knew to hear its glory

These were the men clambering at dawn
among tiered platforms and galleries
built around this slumbering creature
the first to spot the headlines
to read the world upside down and backward
They knew the monster well and knew
to wait and knew to hear its glory

THE HANDS

Taking the Picture: Yousuf Karsh

It was 1951 at the sprawling Ford factory
on Drouillard Road in old Ford City
and there he was fiddling with a large camera
anchored to a tripod, and he stood on the platform
while his wife sat in a nearby chair knitting

– he was studying a forklift driver edging
along a crowded aisle, and suddenly motioned
for the man to brake, then fired off orders
to an assistant to move the lights

and now he sized up the forklift driver
walked over, and swiftly snapped the cigarette
from the factory worker's mouth
suggesting he replace it with a fresh one

then told the driver to take off his cap
tuck it into his back pocket, then summoned
another factory worker to pose in
the foreground –

all of this occupying just a few moments
and meticulous adjustments before
releasing the shutter –

'

Karsh remembered those early days –
blue-collar neighbourhoods near
the plants and foundries, and the union men

called them *men of brawn with arms*
like steel bands and chests like great casks
… fathers, husbands, proud of their wives
and children … Immigrants, like myself …

Years later, I asked what he looked for
in a portrait, the magic, the defining
moment in capturing that person
and without hesitation, and lifting
his hands to frame his thoughts said –
I look at you, the slope of your shoulders and back
as you lean over that notebook, your hand moving
rhythmically as you write down what I tell you
and I see a writer listening, working …
I have the picture … It is you.

Hands of a Saint: Mother Teresa

The first thing I noticed were her fingernails
nicely trimmed, rounded, buffed,
hands, larger than I imagined, resting on her lap
the white gown and blue stripes
accentuating the dark slender fingers

and suddenly she was fidgeting, wringing
her hands, almost as if she were trying
to avoid me but she was distracted
by the movement and clatter
of delicate china plates and cups and saucers
being arranged on long wooden tables
in the basement of this Detroit church

and all around her
women moved swiftly, hurrying
for the civic dignitaries upstairs –
there to be seen, to mark the opening
of Mother's new Cass Corridor mission

Not sure why I fixated on the nails
or her hands but I knew stories of her –

fingers tracing simple lessons in the sand
for children, instructing them to be kind
to one another, the same crooked fingers picking

maggots from wounds of people suffering
in the streets of Calcutta, rough sturdy hands
embracing bright faces of young boys and girls
and praising God for blessings of being alive

but the nails –
manicured, gleaming, perfect in every way

Mickey Mantle's Last At Bat at Tiger Stadium

I remember that day, Sept. 19, 1968 –
I was sitting at a lunch counter at a Coney Island joint
on Lafayette in downtown Detroit, just minutes
from Tiger Stadium and the radio carried
the mellifluous voice of Ernie Harwell – one out
and nobody on the bases, Tigers in the lead 6-1
top of the 8th inning and coming to the plate
the great Mickey Mantle, and on the mound
the cocky Detroit right-hander Denny McLain
who was cruising to his 31st win

and what happened next nobody knows for sure
except for maybe McLain, but Mantle signaled
for a fastball, letter high, and McLain standing
tall on the mound – his cap yanked down
shading his eyes – peered up to get a better look
like someone wearing bifocals
and he nodded slowly

and the next thing you knew was the delivery
of a tailor-made pitch, and the ball sailed
like a rocket into the right-field seats – a spoon-fed
535th career homer, packaged up with a ribbon
laced around it and a message loud and clear
There you go! No need to ask twice

Years later, I talked with McLain at a Detroit
radio station – he was nearly 300 pounds
his famous right hand now like a machine crushing
and slamming one tin coke can after another
and tossing them into a nearby pail
all through the broadcast

and I spoke with him another time right after
he got out of jail and was slinging, not fastballs
but slurpees at 7-11 and once more I asked:
Do you remember that day with Mantle?" And again
he smiled. *"C'mon, I was 24!"* But not before
simultaneously and quietly flashing that steely gaze
of a pitcher, chin tucked down, and his big
right hand in slow motion lobbing a fake pitch

Jimmy Sleeps Alone

I saw him once at the *Mercury Bar* in Detroit
— there he was, mouth running off and
arms and hands waving all about
above a fat burger on a plate

and it surprised me he only ever drank soda
and never smoked and there he was after
a Tigers game, sitting alone, chatting up
a waiter, and I couldn't believe my eyes

– there he was the Teamster boss yammering
in his last days in Detroit, and later I read
how the day he went missing he telephoned
his wife Josephine from a payphone to say

he'd been stood up at a lunch meeting
and so the story goes – two mobsters dumped
him into a 55-gallon drum, and loaded him
onto a truck and drove him to New Jersey

Others claim he's buried beneath the RenCen
and for years, Detroiters trekked to a local bakery
to scoop up "Jimmy Hoffa cupcakes" decorated
with a zombie hand sticking out of the icing

No matter what, Detroiters keep digging for him
in backyards, under foundations, new building sites
but *Jimmy sleeps alone,* and I know for a while
after his sudden disappearance, I struggled

to recall what he'd been mumbling at the *Mercury*
and swear I never killed Jimmy Hoffa, and I swear
he isn't buried in my backyard in Windsor –
the city dug up the sewer lines last spring

On Meeting Benjamin Spock

The sunlight silhouetted him that day
at the dusty corner at Grand Circus Park, and
I saw him, a stooped tall old man wearing
a white shirt, sleeves rolled tightly up his forearms
and he was surveying the towering city, possibly
curious over the way the morning light slanted
and sliced across its vertical shapes and I noticed him

start a conversation with a nearby fellow with a broom
sweeping the street, and soon the two were paused
and chatting in what looked important, what seemed
serious or urgent yet it was likely nothing
maybe the weather, maybe about the *Tigers*
maybe about nothing at all, and that's when
I crossed the street to meet him

and he told me to take a look at how the soaring
buildings were, all at different heights, up and down
straight and tall, like Lego pieces, he said, an imaginary
urban landscape, and the man with the broom
nodded decisively, and said it wasn't *imaginary*
– *I build one of those every day for my youngest*
and the old man with the white shirt laughed

and smacked his forehead, his right-hand flashing
an open wrinkled palm and said – *there you go –*
and it's true – you never know what you're capable of
and the man with the broom beamed – *Yeah,*
I do know. I build a city every night and
some buildings come tumbling down and I know
I can put them right back up

I think of that man on the streets of Detroit
his thoughts ranging all over the map how
perhaps he was dead wrong about raising kids
but the bottom line meant forgetting the rules
when it came to 'love' when it came to 'feelings'
that mattered and that's why he took up the cause
of American kids parading off to meaningless wars

The Hands: Muhammad Ali

The hands I noticed first –
I sat down across from him
knowing the swagger
and bluster and swiftness
and now before me
he moved with aching slowness
not with the grace of history

still, his words were in perfect timing
slow, yet ever calculating
not surprising – they always were that way

still, it was always the mouth that worked the room
with hands following in rabbit jabs
– a flash and blur of fists punching
the air, punctuating the poetry

That day there was none of that –
his words sadly emptied into silence
– hands moved in a mime of slow motion

or so I thought –
when all at once he took me by surprise
his left hand suddenly soared and swiped
the air above my head

I felt myself ducking
but it was his mouth that championed
the moment – as it always did
– that self-satisfied beaming smile
breaking across his handsome mug

Arthur Miller: Don't Ask?

The first thing he said was
Don't ask me about Marilyn
so we parlayed about everything else
university days in Michigan
writing for the student newspaper
of course, *Death of a Salesman*
its opening on Broadway in 1949
winning a Pulitzer –

really it was only Marilyn we wanted
what that wedding day was like
him in your shirtsleeves, cutting the cake
smiling and talking a mile a minute
and there she was – a white apparition
all beauty, all purity, all silence
as news photographers leaned in to snap away
the splendor of that moment

And what did she say when he told her
she could roll into a party like a grenade
and wreck complacent couples with a smile?
What did she say? And was it true
about her going to the cemetery the day
before her aunt's funeral – she was 14
and asked the men digging the grave
if she could climb down the ladder

while they stood around leaning
on their shovels, and she lay on the cold ground
gazing up at a cloudless sky, and what
was it like to hear such stories and the time
in Boston, her showing up at a diner
wearing a bulky heavy cable-knit sweater
a checkered woolen skirt and moccasins
and not a single soul recognizing her?

And why did she insist upon calling you Papa?
I asked. *What was that all about?*

Tomato Wine

for Al Purdy

I drove all one late afternoon back home
from Ameliasburgh, bottles of tomato wine
clinking in the cardboard boxes
in the trunk of my car

a toddler crying in the back seat, a young
daughter daydreaming, and my wife and I
fishtailing the back roads that hot summer day
hauling the tomato wine that Al made

and made us take with us when we left
his A-frame on Roblin Lake, even though
I swore there was no room, but he found
a way to wedge the boxes into the car

and so I carried the bottles back to our place
and stored them in the basement and
they stayed there, year after year, never
uncorked or tried, and though I grumbled

I wouldn't throw them out, in fact, when
we moved, the cardboard boxes and
two dozen bottles of tomato wine made their way
with everything else, and once again

they were stored in my basement and stayed
there for years, sometimes being shuffled
from one corner to another, and never once
were opened, till finally one day in a moment

of clarity, or reckless abandon, whatever
I gathered up the broken cardboard boxes
of tomato wine and placed them gently in the backseat
of my car and drove them to the dump

and couldn't help but duck down as I sped away
somehow suspecting to find Al, shirtsleeves rolled
tightly up to the elbows and cursing up a storm for
how we had just wasted a good batch of homemade wine

Postcard from Paris:
Afternoon with Mavis Gallant

I half expected a place reflecting somehow
the advertisements from the *New Yorker*
where she published her stories
but as it turned out the day I went to meet her
we sat in a poky little kitchen, the Paris rooftops
of Montparnasse nodding all around me, looking
almost as if they knew something I didn't
and weren't about to tell me

and I watched her making coffee the whole time
peppering me with questions, eager to know
the stories I wrote for the paper, what I was doing
in Paris and also wondered if my wife was
going shopping, and if so, *Avoid Galerie Lafayette
And I'll tell you the best spots* she said, then
reached for a tattered green notebook and tore out
a page and scrawled out names and addresses

Five years later in mid-September 1986, I received
a postcard from Paris, an awkward apology from the writer
confessing how awful she felt over suggesting my wife
might find great *deals* at Tati's on Rue de Rennes –
the bargain store just around the corner from her flat
where terrorists had just tossed a bomb from a passing car
killing five, injuring 50, an aftermath of
broken glass and blood and headless mannequins

Joni Mitchell's Bed

I slept in her bed

That's another story

I spotted her at the *Riverboat*
emerging in the wee hours –
daylight still asleep and she
was stepping out with
a guitar case, and pushing back
her blond hair, and she smiled
almost as if she knew me

or perhaps I only imagined that
but as I made my way home
I only wish I could've said
something cool, something
anything – instead I kept walking
but yes, I turned to look again
her figure silhouetted by
Yorkville's lamp lights

a brightening blond halo
evaporating in the stillness
and darkness of early morning

Walking in Thomas Merton's Boots

for Brother Paul Quenon at the Abbey of Gethsemani

The field outside the hermitage is soggy
with January rain rendering my street shoes
useless and so I reach for a pair of rubber
boots by the door only to find three
left-fitting galoshes, one right. Someone's
walked off with two rights or so it would appear
What's with this place? Everything's labelled
Merton's Water, Merton's Gloves, Merton's Ax
Everything else must be mine. Who is this Merton?
A question he probably needed to answer himself
It occurs to me as I shove my feet into
the rubber boots and step out into the dampness
leaving behind two lefts that Merton's out there
somewhere – trudging around with two
right-fitting boots marked legibly *Merton's Boots*.

Finding the Right Words: Robert Giroux

He had been a close friend, a schoolmate
and his editor, and long after the famous monk's death
he still made the trip from New York to Kentucky
to the monastery, and as always
in the morning would go out with his cane
and walk among the simple white crosses
on the slope beside the church
where Thomas Merton was buried
and pause at his friend's marker
even during the winter, stopping to say
something under a smoke-gray sky –
for him, it was all part of an endless
conversation though mostly it continued
in silence but for the wind sweeping like
the holy spirit across the stone walls bordering
the monastery, nudging him to move on
For him there were memories, and certainly
what he read between the lines of the poems
and essays and diaries, all the words that once
made perfect sense in another time
That was enough to bring him back –
to have dinner with the monks, venture out
to the hermitage in the woods, a place to write
and pray and hear the howl and yip of coyotes at night

Sleeping Beauty: Karen Kain

The moment I saw her, she was wearing
black leotards, and sitting on a studio floor
in Detroit, and she sighed and stared down
at her ballet slippers, slowly shook her head
glanced up, eyes meeting mine, then rose
long straight legs moving with grace
but her stride, and the look on her face
spoke, *I don't want to talk*

I can't recall really what she said
– though my tape recorder does

I know in between the stream of words
there was so much more of how she felt –
all the attention on her meant everyone else
missing the moment, the beauty, and
I missed that too in the way she stood
legs crossed at an angle, but the shape
of her glowing amidst a room of arms and legs
of young ballerinas, all in a blur
of movement, of colour, of space, of time

Instead, I heard, *I don't want to talk, I don't
want to talk, I don't want to talk* and missed the point
about all that was real – it wasn't about her
it was about beauty and grace

I missed it all

Belonging Somewhere: Rosa Parks

I noticed her –
sitting in a corner waiting for Mother Teresa
waiting for this saint to make her way
down those wooden steps
and leave behind the hallelujahs

to embrace Detroit's Cass Corridor,
soup kitchens, single mothers, the homeless

I went over, and she smiled
and after a few moments nodded tiredly
to the same story she's told
a million times before
all about that commute home after
working all day as a seamstress
and settling into a seat
in the coloured section of
that Montgomery Alabama bus
and refusing to give it up
to a white man

It was the winter of 1955
and there was nothing that was going
to budge Rosa from that comfortable seat

Now she rested beside me on a wooden chair
in the basement of this church –
hands folded over her knees
happy at escaping all the formal liturgy
from the sanctuary above

not the least bit impatient to meet Mother Teresa

The bus story finished abruptly
and Rosa waved a hand for me to let it rest –
she's told it so many times before
so I changed the topic
How about them Tigers?

and her face brightened, and she muffled a giggle
and soon the focus was the neighbourhood
– the mission Mother Teresa was starting

Her battles will never end it seems
– they've been a part of her fabric growing up
memories in the south of a grandfather
pacing in front of their house with a shotgun
as the Ku Klux Klan marched by

nightmares still of a white man next door
trying to rape her and in all the wildness
she was thinking *If he wanted to kill me*
and rape a dead body, he was welcome
but he'd have to kill me first

activism in seeking justice for black victims
of white brutality and sexual violence
openly calling Malcolm X her personal hero

but I didn't see this in this quiet woman
seated in a church basement
amid a broken-down landscape of crack houses
and burned-out shells of buildings

I saw uncertainty over what
she was going to tell Mother Teresa
because no one else knew the neighbourhood
knew the people by name
knew their struggles

yet everybody knew her

As I got up to leave, Rosa looked up
and I saw it still there in her eyes
– all that fire and tenacity
simmering and alive

yet the truth was in her own words
about the loneliness of being a rebel

I am nothing. I belong nowhere

The One Thing that Catches the Eye:
Mary Ellen Mark

Every afternoon she excused herself
tucked a satchel under her arm, and turned
and offered a limp wave, and was gone –
every day a blood transfusion at a nearby clinic

this legendary photographer whose modest gesture
was as simple and straightforward as her pictures
Keep it simple, find the one spot that catches the eye
and it was that *idea* that transformed the moment

She was dying, but wasn't giving up –
and in Palm Springs that May 2015 she gathered
a group of students around her and told them
photography meant *Letting it happen*

backing away, and permitting the image to come to life
as she did with stories of runaway kids, women
in prisons, the mentally ill, teenage prostitutes,
– finding a way into those moments, letting it live

and on the last day at the festival a few
in the audience caught that line when those iconic
pictures lit up the massive screen behind her
as she said *You know, I'll live forever, don't you?*

Three weeks later she died in Manhattan
of a bone and blood marrow disease

Vladimir Horowitz: The American Tour Resumes in Detroit After the Death of His Mother

He was six when his mother slid in beside him
at the piano in the parlour in Kyiv to guide
his hands over the vast array of gleaming black
and white keys, and now the warm glow
of a single-stage light enveloped
the imposing nine-foot Steinway that brooded
like a *Toro Bravo* in the Iberian sunlight

and there he was – a tall yet short-waisted man
walking slowly to the edge of the stage to pause
and bow and tell his audience this performance
would be for his mother, his first piano teacher

I didn't notice right away when he turned briskly
to move to the piano bench and sit all the way
to one side – ungainly and not perfectly lined up
but then again, his hands always tilted down
palms slightly below the level of the Steinway's
gleaming Bavarian spruce keys, nearly cupping
the edge, playing chords with straight fingers
and always the little finger of his right hand
it was said, curiously curled up and ready
to strike like a cobra – I didn't notice
until he had started in, and then spotted
that awkward gap, the place beside him, empty

but now for the ghost of his mother taking
her young boy through the moment
guiding him in all the radiance of his return

EPILOGUE

Obits

Every morning I scoop up the paper
from between the doors of my house
spread the pages out on the kitchen table
a steaming mug of tea beside
and check out each one of the obits
scan the names to see if I recognize anybody

This isn't something that comes with old age
or fear of missing out about old friends
passing away and never sending flowers
– I've always done this, a practice from
my days as a reporter, the first impulse
in the morning reading through the obits

then telephoning funeral homes to see
if anyone of public prominence had died
and from there we'd collect details –
family phone numbers, dig through the "morgue"
the name we gave to our archives
and bit by bit type out a story for the editor

Now the practice has turned to imagining –
piecing together another story, finding a twist
of plots with dialogue and mystery and irony
wondering which of the children or grandchildren
will take over the company, run for political office
or even wind up embezzling the family fortune

Acknowledgements

GETTING SOMEONE TO PICK UP and read your work is the biggest acknowledgement. At the top of that list is Bruce Meyer, who spent the time shaping and organizing this manuscript, and writing his introduction. He was my guide. Michael Mirolla is another who put his faith in publishing this work. John B. Lee was also there for every one of these poems. The two of us regularly trade poem for poem, each harassing the other with something new that we have written. But as I say, the list is endless of others to whom I owe by gratitude for the support of my work. To name a few, let me include Peter Hrastovec, Ted Kloske, Howard and Jeannette Aster, Vanessa Shields, André Narbonne, Douglas MacLellan, Keith Carter, Phil Hall, Laurence Hutchman, Terry Ann Carter, Mary Ann Mulhern, Christopher Lawrence Menard, Micheline Maylor, Susan McMaster, Rosemary Sullivan and Karen Mulhallen. Of course, my own family – they listen when they don't have to.

About the Author

MARTY GERVAIS is a Canadian poet, photographer, journalist, and teacher. He has won many literary awards including the prestigious Toronto's Harbourfront Festival Prize for his contributions to Canadian letters and to emerging writers, the Milton Acorn People's Poetry Award, and the City of Windsor's Mayor's Award. Gervais is also the recipient of 16 Western Ontario Newspaper Awards for journalism. He was Windsor's inaugural Poet Laureate, and is now Poet Laureate Emeritus.

Printed in January 2022
by Gauvin Press,
Gatineau, Québec